Olneyville Library - PCL

 O9-AIF-101

DISCARDED

THIS CANDLEWICK BOOK BELONGS TO:

_____

_____

_____

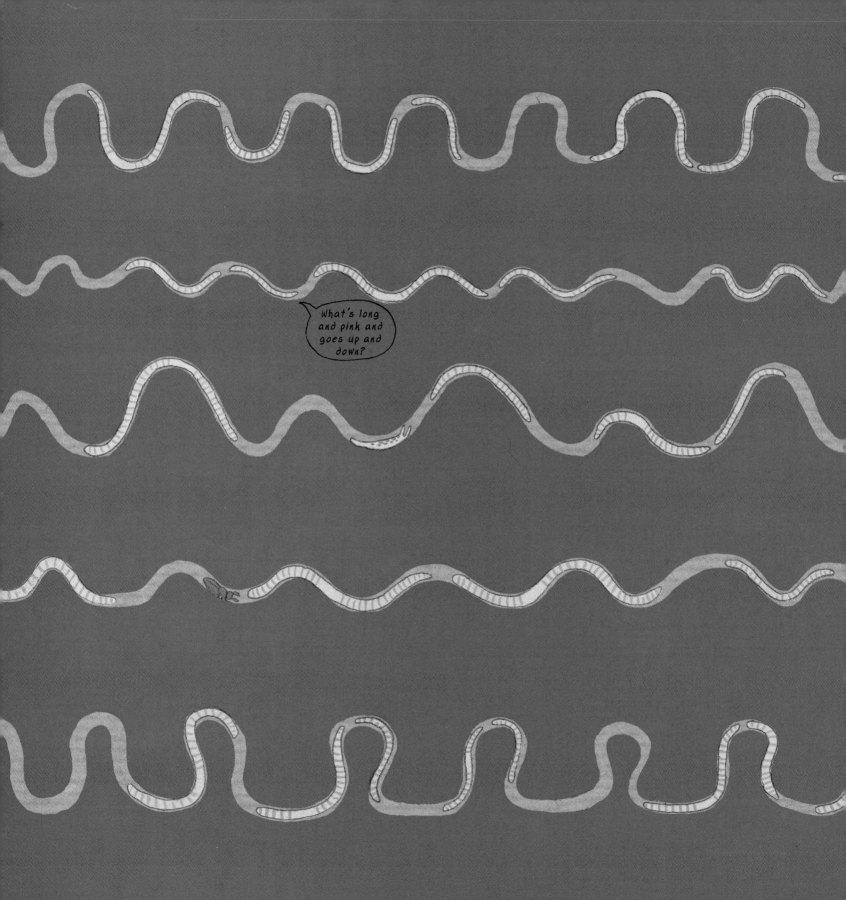

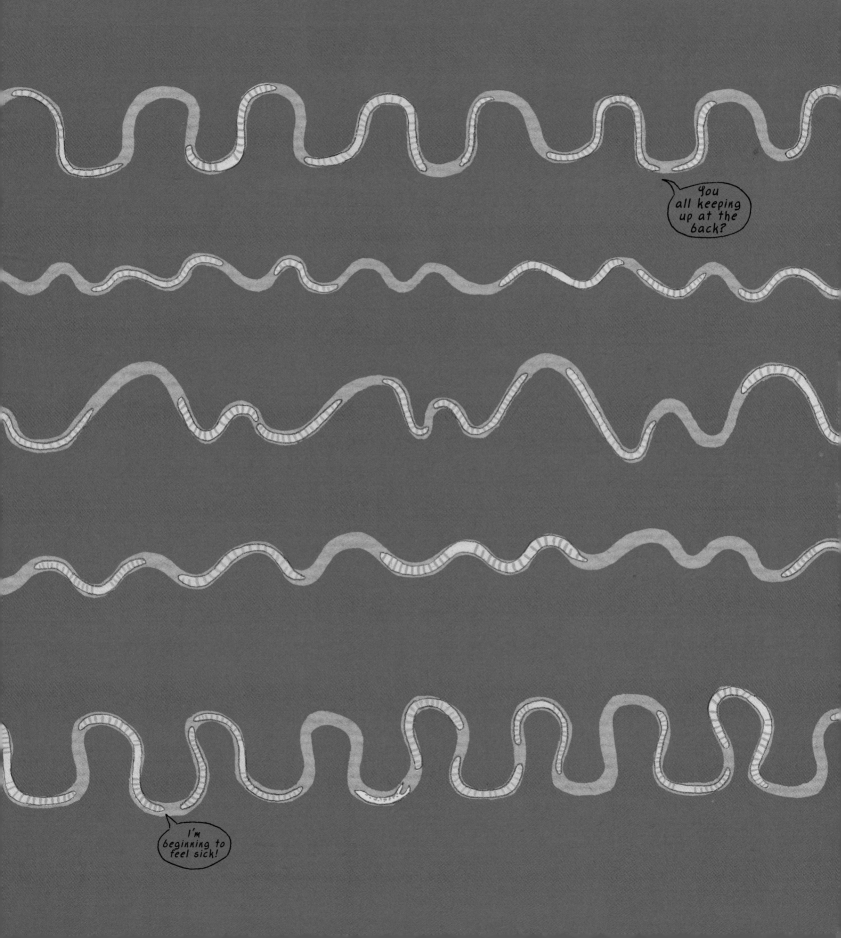

Providence Community Library

3 1357 00162 5646
YUCKY WORMS

MAY 31 2013

Text copyright © 2009 by Vivian French
Illustrations copyright © 2009 by Jessica Ahlberg

All rights reserved. No part of this book may be reproduced, transmitted,
or stored in an information retrieval system in any form or by any means,
graphic, electronic, or mechanical, including photocopying, taping, and
recording, without prior written permission from the publisher.

First U.S. paperback edition 2012

The Library of Congress has cataloged the hardcover edition as follows:
French, Vivian.
Yucky worms / Vivian French ; illustrated by Jessica Ahlberg. — 1st U.S. ed.
p. cm.
Summary: While helping Grandma in the garden, a child learns about the
important role of the earthworm in helping plants grow.
ISBN 978-0-7636-4446-8 (hardcover)
[1. Earthworms — Fiction. 2. Gardening — Fiction. 3. Grandmothers — Fiction.] I.
Ahlberg, Jessica, ill. II. Title.
PZ7.F88917Yu 2010
[E] — dc22
2009017307

ISBN 978-0-7636-5817-5 (paperback)

13 14 15 16 CCP

2 3 4 5 6 7 8 9 10

Printed in Shenzhen, Guangdong, China

This book was typeset in Marker Finepoint and Providence.
The illustrations were done in pencil and gouache.

Candlewick Press
99 Dover Street
Somerville, Massachusetts 02144

visit us at www.candlewick.com

For Jack
V. F.

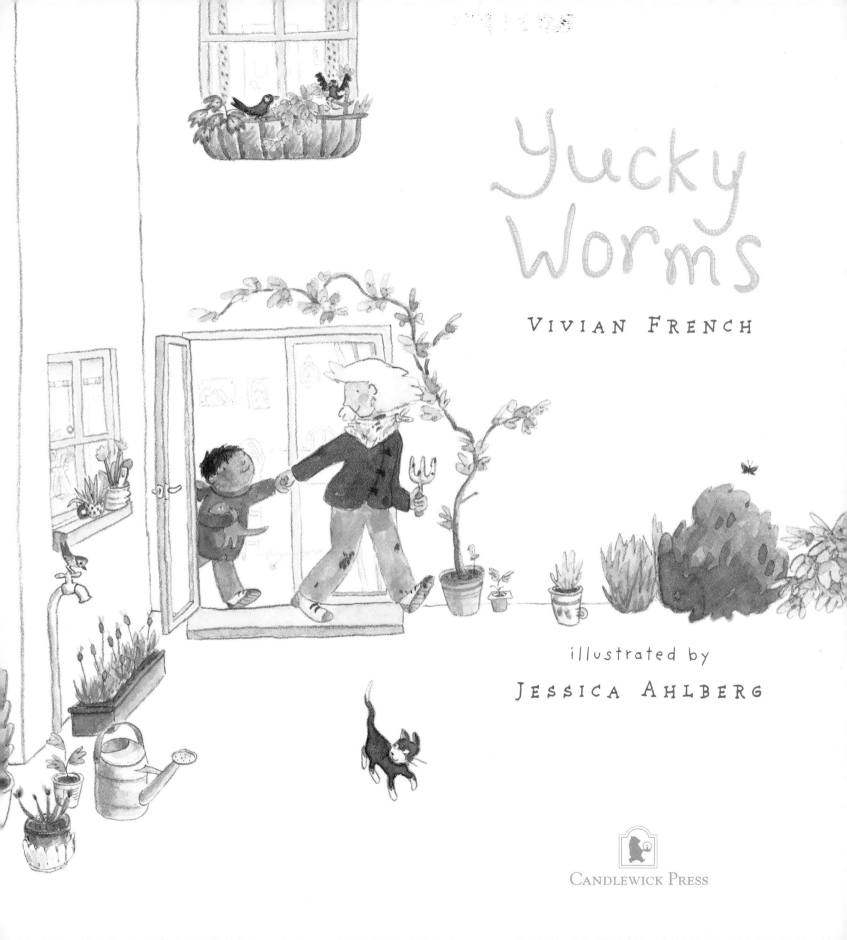

Yucky Worms

VIVIAN FRENCH

illustrated by

JESSICA AHLBERG

CANDLEWICK PRESS

One day when I was
in Grandma's garden,
Grandma dug up a slimy,

slithery,

wiggly

worm.

"Yuck!" I said. "Throw it away!"

"Throw it away?" Grandma looked horrified.

"Would you throw away one of your friends?"

"You can't be friends with a worm," I said.

"You can't even tell which end is which."

"Yes, you can! Watch."
Grandma put the worm down.

It gave a kind of
squirmy wriggle
and disappeared
really fast,
pointy end first.

As the rounded end vanished,
Grandma said, "There goes its tail."
I bent down to look, and I could see
it had left a little tunnel.

IN MOST BACKYARDS
THERE WILL BE ABOUT
FIFTEEN WORMS IN EVERY
SQUARE YARD OF SOIL.

"Where did it go?" I asked.
"Home," Grandma said.
"It's an earthworm.
It lives underground."

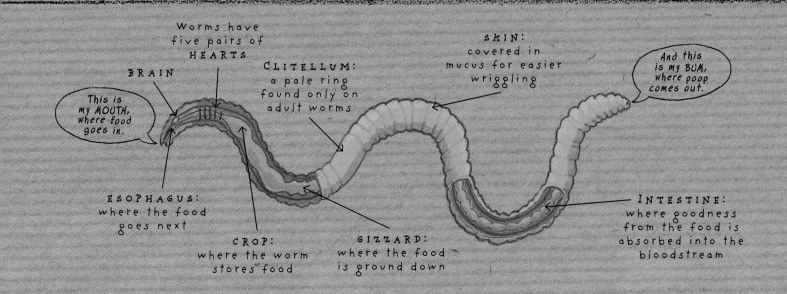

Worms have
five pairs of
HEARTS

BRAIN

This is
my MOUTH,
where food
goes in.

CLITELLUM:
a pale ring
found only on
adult worms

SKIN:
covered in
mucus for easier
wriggling

And this
is my BUM,
where poop
comes out.

ESOPHAGUS:
where the food
goes next

CROP:
where the worm
stores food

GIZZARD:
where the food
is ground down

INTESTINE:
where goodness
from the food is
absorbed into the
bloodstream

"But what does it eat? Dirt?"
I wanted to know.
"It eats tiny, tiny stones and bits of dirt,"
Grandma told me, "but worms eat other things
too, like rotting leaves
and flowers and fruit and dead insects.
They especially like eating at night,
when it's cool.

Mmm, moldy.

Dirt is good for you.

YUCK! Can't eat this.

10

WORMS COME ABOVE
GROUND TO FIND
THINGS TO
EAT TOO.

Nice
and rotten.
Just how I
like it.

THEY PULL
THEIR FOOD
BACK DOWN
AS THEY WRIGGLE
INTO THE
GROUND AGAIN.

The stones and dirt help to grind
everything up in the worm's stomach,
and then the worm
poops it back out."

Zzzzz.

11

Grandma pointed
at the flowerbed.
"LOOK! Can you see?"
I bent down—and I saw
what looked like a weird,
long curly worm made of dirt.
"That's worm poop," Grandma said. "It's called a cast.
You know when you recycle things? Well, worms
do it too. There's still a lot of goodness
left in the things a worm eats, and when the
goodness comes out again as poop, it helps
plants to grow BIG and STRONG.
And as the worms move around, under and on top of the soil,
the poop gets spread around the garden."

"That's why
worms are my friends."
Grandma gave me a thumbs-up.
"And it's not just their poop
that's good for plants.
The tunnels they dig
loosen the soil—so
roots can stretch out and
air and rainwater
can get in."

WORMS' POOP IS SO FINE AND CR... IT NEVER BLOCKS THEIR TUNNELS.

"That was close!"

"But it's dangerous being a worm . . ." Grandma said.

I stared at her.

"DANGEROUS?" I asked.

She smiled at me.

"Lots and lots of animals think worms make the most delicious dinner.

SHOPPING LIST
WORM
WORM
WORM
WORM

There's a mole over there!

Bird alert!

Birds LOVE them—and

so do moles, badgers, frogs,

hedgehogs, and foxes—even some slugs eat worms.

And human beings accidentally slice through them with spades

and spike them with forks—it's a tough life."

"Cutting them in half doesn't hurt them, Grandma," I said.

"They just turn into two worms and keep on growing."

Grandma shook her head. "Poor worms.

Lots of people think that, but it's not true."

She put her fork down.

"Time for a snack!"

A WORM'S TAIL CAN REGROW IF IT'S CUT OFF, BUT CUTTING A WORM IN HALF WILL KILL IT.

I think I'll hide down here.

17

Grandma had tea, and I had orange juice.
"Can I dig up a worm?" I asked.
"If it rains," Grandma said, "the worms
will come up on their own."

WORMS BREATHE THROUGH THEIR SKINS.
THEY DON'T MIND THE SOIL AROUND THEM BEING WET,
BUT IF THEIR TUNNELS ARE FLOODED, THEY COME UP
TO THE SURFACE TO MOVE AROUND MORE EASILY.

I took a cookie. "What if it doesn't rain?"
Grandma winked at me. "We'll use
the watering can and pretend."
I finished my cookie as fast as I could.
"Can we trick the worms NOW?"

Grandma filled the
watering can,
and I watered
the ground.
Then I stood back—
I didn't want worms
chewing at my shoes.

"They only put their
heads out," Grandma promised.
"And it'll be a while
before they do."

WHEN IT'S
VERY HOT AND
THE SOIL GETS
TOO DRY TO
SLITHER THROUGH . . .

Phew!

A WORM WILL
WRIGGLE DOWN TO
WHERE THE
SOIL IS
STILL DAMP,
CURL UP, AND
WAIT FOR RAIN.

That's
better.

Ooh!
Cozy!

WHEN IT'S VERY COLD, A WORM
WILL WRIGGLE DOWN EVEN DEEPER,
BELOW THE FROST LEVEL, AND CURL
UP WITH OTHER WORMS FOR WARMTH.

Grandma was right. I had time to eat
two more cookies before she said,
"Look!"

"WOW," I said.
I could just see the tip of
a worm above the ground.
"Now watch this."
Grandma stamped her foot,
and the worm disappeared.

"Did it see you?" I asked.
Grandma shook her head.
"Worms don't have eyes.
They feel vibrations,
though—and a thump
like that might mean
a hungry bird is landing.
DANGER!"

Grandma dug her fork in the ground. Up came lots of dirt and wriggly worms. She picked one up and washed it in the watering can.

"Mustn't drop it," she said. "They can't swim."

A WORM HAS RIDGED MUSCLES ALL ALONG ITS BODY.

TO MOVE, IT PUSHES ITS FRONT END FORWARD,

AND USES ITS BRISTLES TO HOLD THAT END IN PLACE WHILE THE BACK CATCHES UP.

Wow, LOOK at those bristles!

Grandma put the clean worm on some paper and held it near my ear. I could hear a tiny rustling noise. "What's that?" "They're covered in little bristles," Grandma said. "The bristles and their muscles help them move."

THE BRISTLES ON THE BACK END KEEP THE WORM FROM SLIDING BACKWARD, WHILE THE FRONT END TUNNELS FORWARD AGAIN INTO THE EARTH.

Away I go!

"I've got muscles too!"
I bent my arm so Grandma could see.

"If you've got so many muscles," she said,
"maybe you'd like to help me plant my
sunflower seedlings?"
"OK," I agreed, and then I thought
of something.

"When I go to school on Monday, I'm going to say that I've got lots of new friends!"

"Good idea," Grandma said.

"But," I said, "I might not actually say they're *worms*."

27

HOW TO BE A WORMOLOGIST!

LOOK FOR:

* worm casts in your garden or in the park

* leaves sticking up out of the ground

* worms on the surface after it rains

EXPERIMENT BY:

* watering a dry patch of grass or dirt and watching to see if worms come up

* tapping on the ground to see if you can make a worm believe it's raining

* carefully digging up a forkful of dirt and counting how many worms you find

A WORM IN THE HAND . . .

*When you pick up a worm, remember to be respectful;
a worm is a living creature.*

** Check how it feels. Is it smooth? Is it slimy?
Can you feel the bristles?
* Watch how it moves.
* Is it a youngster or an adult? (Adults have
a clitellum—a yellow ring around their body.)
* Put the worm back on newly dug soil
and watch how it wriggles away.*

Always wash your hands after touching worms.

Index

Look up the pages
to find out about
all these wormy things.
Don't forget to
look at both kinds
of word—
this kind
and
THIS KIND.

*

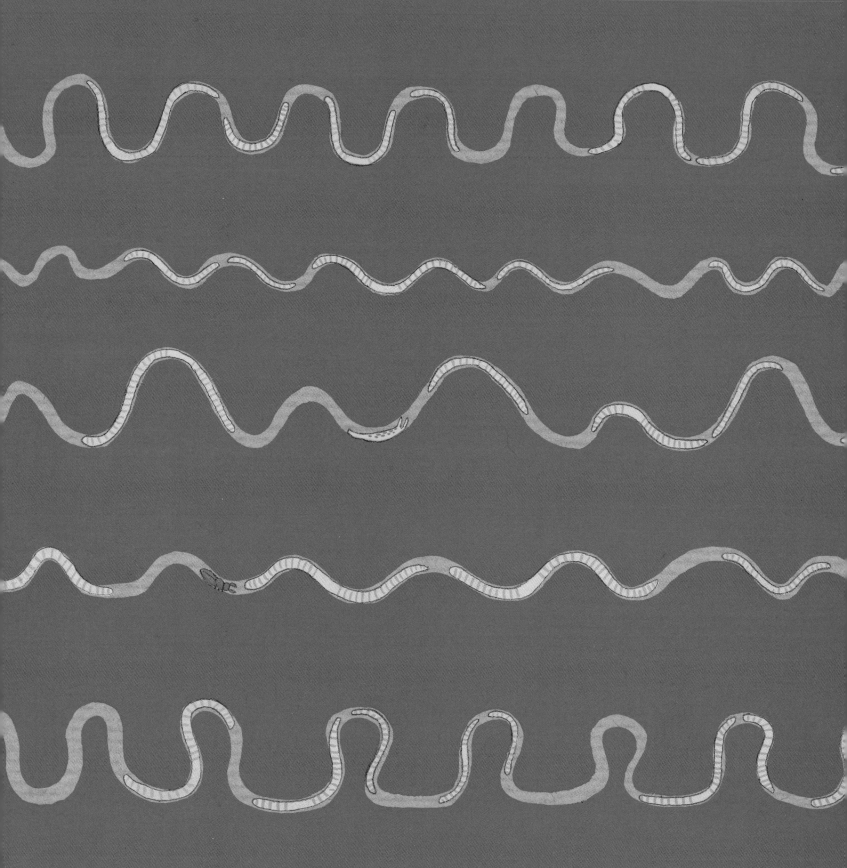